Author's Note

Elephants originated in North Africa 55 million years ago. Over time, scientists have identified more than 300 species in the elephant family. Today, there are thought to be just two★ surviving species: the African elephant, classified as vulnerable, and the Asian elephant, classified as endangered.

These enormous, long-nosed animals have been admired by humans, even worshipped, across time and cultures. Humans have also put elephants to work, carrying heavy loads, fighting wars, performing in circuses, and entertaining tourists. Nowadays, we have come to understand that keeping elephants captive can be very damaging for them, both mentally and physically.

Even in the wild, elephants are in danger from humans. As we cut down forests and develop land for palm oil, farming, and settlement, elephants are losing their essential habitat and historic migration routes. When elephants and humans cross paths, it can be hazardous for both sides. Elephants are also hunted and killed for the ivory of their tusks. Despite the fact that it's illegal, poachers still sell ivory on the black market for jewelry, carvings, and medicines.

Elephants are social, emotional creatures that develop deep bonds within their families. If elephants are to stay healthy and flourish, we must commit to caring for them and protecting the land they need to survive.

★ It is under debate whether African forest elephants, often considered a sub-species, are in fact a third species of elephant in their own right, separate from the African savanna elephant.

For David who never forgets,
with love

My thanks to Holly Rosier, for her time and expert advice on the
African elephant; to Caitlin Melidonis of Elephant Family for her expertise
in Asian elephants; to Karin Snelson for her great care;
and to Claudia Bedrick, my publisher.

The illustrations in this book were created with
watercolor, acrylic, pencil, crayons, and drypoint.

This book is printed on recycled paper.

www.enchantedlion.com

First edition, published in 2018 by Enchanted Lion Books,
67 West Street, Studio 317A, Brooklyn, NY 11222
Text and Illustrations copyright © 2018 by Jenni Desmond
www.jennidesmond.com
Edited by Karin Snelson and Claudia Bedrick
Design & layout: Elliot Kreloff and Marc Drumwright
All rights reserved under International and Pan-American Copyright Conventions
A CIP record is on file with the Library of Congress. ISBN 978-1-59270-264-0
Printed in China in July 2018 by RR Donnelley Asia Printing Solutions Ltd.
3 5 7 9 10 8 6 4 2

THE ELEPHANT

JENNI DESMOND

ENCHANTED LION BOOKS

NEW YORK

Once upon a time, a child took a book from the shelf and started to read...

He read that the elephant is the biggest land mammal in the world, and that elephants are highly intelligent, with extraordinary memories. Even in vast, empty stretches of desert, they are able to remember exactly where they found food and water many years ago.

AFRICA

AFRICAN
FOREST
ELEPHANT

AFRICAN
SAVANNA
ELEPHANT

RAINFORESTS
OR WOODLANDS

OPEN SAVANNA
OR "BUSH"

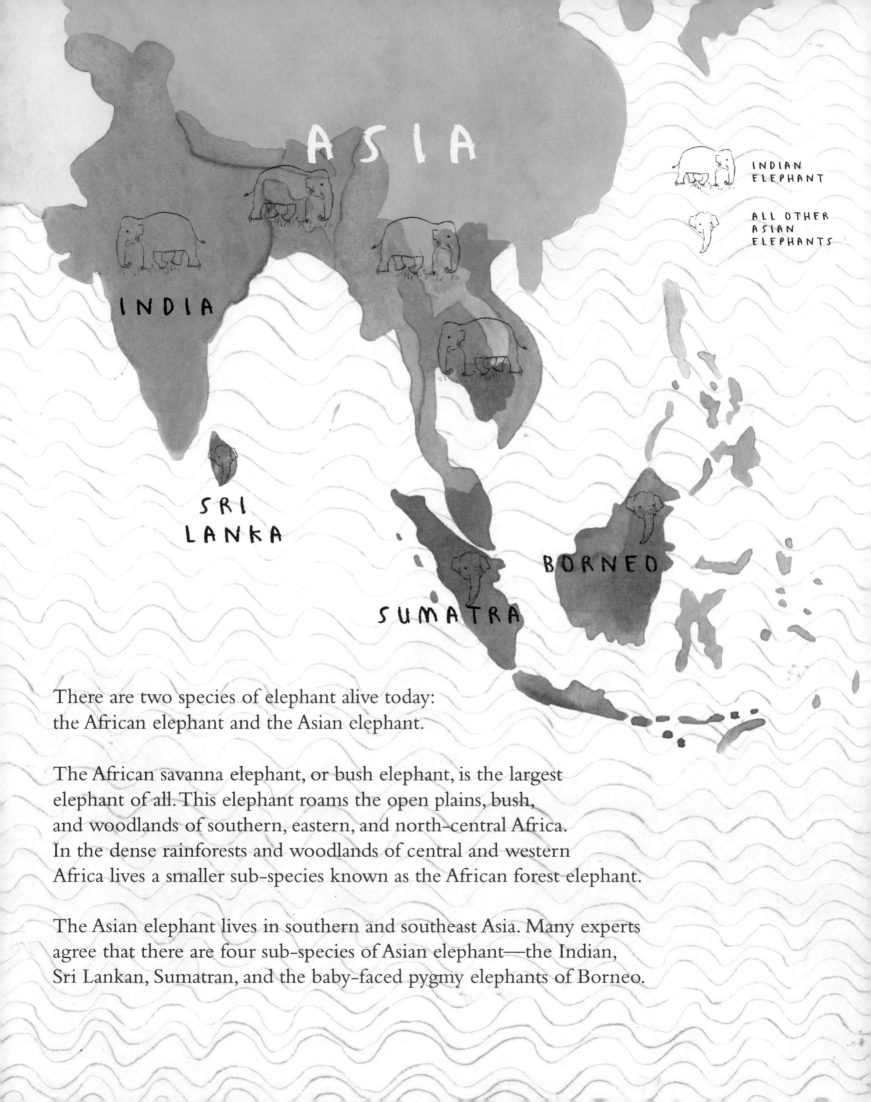

ASIA

INDIAN ELEPHANT

ALL OTHER ASIAN ELEPHANTS

INDIA

SRI LANKA

BORNEO

SUMATRA

There are two species of elephant alive today:
the African elephant and the Asian elephant.

The African savanna elephant, or bush elephant, is the largest
elephant of all. This elephant roams the open plains, bush,
and woodlands of southern, eastern, and north-central Africa.
In the dense rainforests and woodlands of central and western
Africa lives a smaller sub-species known as the African forest elephant.

The Asian elephant lives in southern and southeast Asia. Many experts
agree that there are four sub-species of Asian elephant—the Indian,
Sri Lankan, Sumatran, and the baby-faced pygmy elephants of Borneo.

The many differences between African and Asian elephants make them easy to tell apart, but they are similar, too. Both are massive, yet never clumsy. They are awe-inspiring, yet playful and fun-loving. They are strong, but vulnerable to their constantly changing environment.

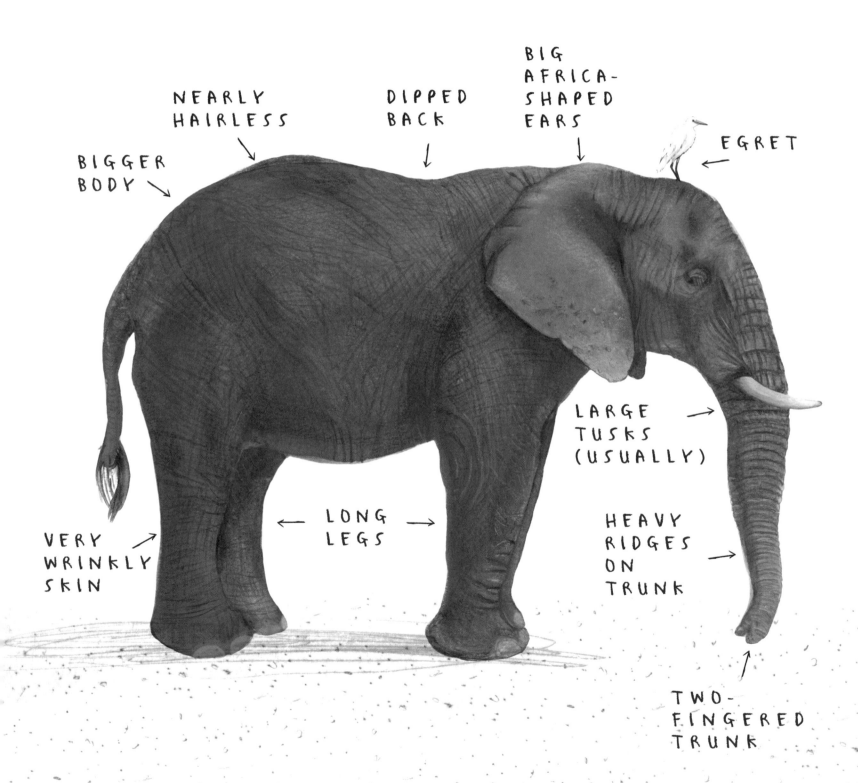

BIGGER BODY

NEARLY HAIRLESS

DIPPED BACK

BIG AFRICA-SHAPED EARS

EGRET

LARGE TUSKS (USUALLY)

VERY WRINKLY SKIN

LONG LEGS

HEAVY RIDGES ON TRUNK

TWO-FINGERED TRUNK

AFRICAN SAVANNA ELEPHANT

All elephants are shades of gray, except when they cover themselves in red, yellow, orange, or brown mud. Their skin is paper-thin around the ears and on other soft spots like the belly, but the skin on their head, back, sides, and legs can be more than an inch thick. No matter how tough and leathery an elephant's skin looks, it is sensitive and full of nerve endings. An elephant can even feel the feet of the tiniest fly landing on its back.

SMALLER LOWER INDIA-SHAPED EARS

TWO-DOMED FOREHEAD

HUMPED BACK

SMALLER BODY

LONG THICK WIRY HAIRS

LESS WRINKLY SKIN THAT TURNS WHITE AND PINK WITH AGE

NOT ALL HAVE TUSKS

SHORTER LEGS

SMOOTHER TRUNK

ONE-FINGERED TRUNK

ASIAN ELEPHANT

An African savanna elephant male, or bull, can reach 13 feet tall and 24 feet long, and can weigh up to seven tons. That's about the weight of four large cars. The females, or cows, are half that size.

Even baby elephants are big. At birth, an African savanna elephant calf can be 260 pounds, the weight of a speedy motor scooter.

Elephants walk on their toes. From the outside, their feet look flat, but inside, the skeleton reveals that the heel is higher than the toes, like a human foot in high heels. A big cushiony pad supports this tiptoe bone structure. This is why elephants appear so graceful and light on their feet, despite their great weight.

The elephant's hefty heel pads muffle the noise of their powerful footfall and make it easier for them to walk on uneven ground. Their spongy feet act as hearing devices too, picking up sound vibrations from as far as six miles away. When an elephant detects a distant elephant, it will freeze and lean forward onto its front feet, listening.

Elephants have excellent hearing. They also use their ears to express emotion. They happily flap them when greeting a friend. Or they might flare them out wide to make themselves look even bigger in the face of danger, such as when an African forest elephant chases away a troublesome leopard.

On hot days, elephants flap their giant ears to cool off, and since some African elephants' ears are as big as full-sized refrigerators, vigorous flapping can generate quite a breeze. This breeze cools the large blood vessels in the thin-skinned ears, and the blood then cools the body.

The elephant's two pointed tusks are long, ivory teeth. Most African elephants—both male and female—have tusks. Male Asian elephants sometimes have tusks, but females never do. If an Asian elephant doesn't have visible tusks, it may instead have two tusk-like incisor teeth called "tushes," which can be seen when its mouth is open.

Tusks keep growing as elephants age, so an old African savanna bull might have tusks that weigh 100 pounds each and measure up to eight feet long, the same length as two seven-year-old children toe to toe.

Elephants use their tusks to dig for edible roots, minerals, and water, to play, to fight, and as a resting place for their tired trunks. Elephants are either left- or right-tusked, so the most-used tusk will wear down first and look shorter than the other.

An elephant's trunk is the longest, most versatile nose in the animal world. Elephants use their flexible trunks—part upper lip, part nose—to smell the air and earth for nearby food and water sources, and to pick up the scent of other elephants or possible danger. They also use their hose-like noses to breathe, drink, eat, trumpet, lift things, spray themselves with dust or water, to play, wrestle, dig, wallop, and to comfort and caress. Elephants may even exchange greetings by putting their trunks inside each other's mouths.

The huge trunk is boneless, but heavy, with 100,000 muscles. Some trunks are so strong they can uproot small trees from the ground. As mighty as it is, the trunk is also sensitive and precise, because all of those muscles give elephants tremendous control. They can pick up the smallest berries or seeds from the ground with the tips of their fingered trunks.

Female elephants—grandmothers, aunties, mothers, cousins, and sisters—most often live their whole lives separate from adult male elephants in a close family group, or herd, of around six to twelve. These families, including young bulls, do everything together. The matriarch is usually the oldest and always the wisest of the group and can live to be 70 years old. She is the leader and protector.

She will have learned from her own mother, or her mother's mother, where to find water in droughts, where the best food is, and which path to take. The younger cows and bulls trust her and follow her lead, stopping when she stops, and sleeping when she decides.

A baby bull lives in the female herd until he becomes a boisterous teenager and begins teasing the other elephants. At that point, the young bull will leave the herd to either wander alone or to join an all-male herd.

Bull elephants do a lot of play-fighting… and real fighting. Their fiercest fights are over females. Males will battle to the death with tusks and trunks, and it's the oldest and largest male that usually wins.

When a male is ready to mate, he is in a very irritable state called "musth." He becomes aggressive, and the glands between his ear and eye stream with smelly liquid. Female elephants can often smell a bull long before they see him. The male will follow his mate's herd for a few days before leaving her to carry and raise the calf without him.

A mother elephant is pregnant with her baby for 22 months—nearly two years—before giving birth. Within an hour after birth, as soon as the calf can stand on its wobbly feet, it begins to feed on its mother's milk from the two teats between her front legs. For the next two to five years, the baby will stay close, rarely straying more than a few feet away from its mother.

The rest of the herd helps raise the youngster for the next ten years, teaching it to use its trunk, showering it with affection, and protecting it from big cats or the blistering hot sun.

Elephants eat almost constantly. Because their vision is weak, these herbivores rely on their strong senses of touch and smell for feeding. The coolest hours of the day and night are the ideal time for elephants to sniff around for grass, leaves, plants, branches, bulbs, seeds, tree bark, shrubs, vegetables, and fruits, all of which they mash up with their four brick-sized molars.

A large male could eat 700 pounds of plant matter a day, the equivalent of 100 apples, 90 lemons, 80 peaches, 70 pears, 60 oranges, 50 mangoes, 40 bananas, 30 coconuts, 20 pineapples, and 15 watermelons. Elephants don't digest their food efficiently, so that same fruit-devouring elephant might poo 12 to 15 times in one day, producing more than 300 pounds of steaming dung.

Elephants need a lot of water and will walk hundreds
of miles to find a good watering hole. They can drink up
to 50 gallons a day, with astonishing speed, by sucking
the water up into their trunks, tilting back their heads, and
pouring it into their mouths. Baby elephants drink
with their mouths instead, because it takes them
almost a year to learn to control their trunks.

Elephants are strong swimmers and use their trunks like snorkels. They love to
splash and play and blow bubbles. To cool off, they wallow in water and mud,
squirting themselves with their trunks. The many wrinkles in their skin help
trap water, allowing them to stay cooler longer on hot days. When mud from
the watering hole dries on their bodies, that layer protects their skin from the
sun and from biting insects.

Elephants thrive when they have plenty of room to roam. As they push and eat their way through forests, elephants clear paths, enabling other hungry animals to feed on the leaves of flattened trees. They also deepen watering holes as they thrash around with their large bodies. Their colossal dung piles help feed other animals, and as elephants migrate, the seeds in their dung spread the growth of acacia trees and other plants.

Elephants are a "keystone species," which means that their existence is uniquely important to other plants and animals.

Many elephants die naturally between the age of 60 and 70, often because they have lost their teeth and can no longer chew solid food. Elephants grow six sets of four molars during their lifetime. Once the last set has fallen out, they will eventually die of hunger.

When an elephant dies, its closest family members may linger next to the body for many days, stroking it with their trunks, touching it with their feet, and covering it with bits of grass, branches, or earth. As the years pass, an elephant will return again and again to the site of the bones. Elephants are also curious about any unfamiliar elephant skeletons they come across and may pause to gently examine them with their trunks.

Wild elephants sleep less than most mammals, sometimes for as little as two hours, or not at all. Matriarchs rarely lie down, as they need to stay on their toes, alert to any danger.

When it's time to go to sleep, all the elephants in a herd will crowd together, often with the larger elephants dozing off while standing up on the outside and the smaller ones lying down in the safety of the middle.

Unlike elephants, people need to sleep all night long.
Sometimes, we might even fall asleep over a favorite book
and begin to dream…